MILLIE'S
BOOK

MILLIE'S

B · O · O · K

As Dictated to Barbara Bush

William Morrow and Company, Inc.
New York

Millie's Book / as dictated to Barbara Bush
    p.   cm.
ISBN 0-688-04033-0
    1. Bush, George, 1924-   —Anecdotes. 2. Millie (Dog) 3. Dogs—
United States—Biography.
E840.8.B87W45   1990
973.928'092—dc20
[B]
                                                        90-5421
                                                        CIP

Printed in the United States of America

First Edition

        4   5   6   7   8   9   10

BOOK DESIGN BY JAYE ZIMET

Bar and I would like to dedicate this book with love to:

Will and Sarah Farish, who brought us together,

Susan Porter Rose, who has supported us in this project and every other project for years,

and

George Bush, whom we both love more than life.

I want to thank the following very special people for their contributions to Millie's Book:

All the photographers who gave their pictures so freely and generously; all those people who were quoted or photographed; and a very special thanks to William Morrow and Company for its contributions to literacy; and to Lisa Drew, my editor, who laughed in all the right places!

—MKB

The mission of The Barbara Bush Foundation for Family Literacy is:

1. *To support the development of family literacy programs* . . . help mobilize the creativity, resources and will of a country as great as America and make it possible for us to take control of our literacy crisis and build a nation of readers by building families of readers.

2. *To break the intergenerational cycle of illiteracy* . . . help provide family learning so parent and child can learn to read together with materials and instruction available to each of them.

3. *To establish literacy as a value in every family in America* . . . help every family in the nation understand that the home is the child's first school, that the parent is the child's first teacher, and that reading is the child's first subject.

The Barbara Bush Foundation for Family Literacy
% The Community Foundation of Greater Washington
1002 Wisconsin Avenue, N.W.
Washington, D.C. 20007
(202) 338-8993

All author proceeds will be donated to
The Barbara Bush Foundation for Family Literacy

MILLIE'S
BOOK

y name is Mildred Kerr Bush and I came to live with the Bush family on February 13, 1987. Their previous dog, C. Fred Bush, had died on January 20, and George, who was then Vice-President of the United States of America, knew that Bar missed him and needed a dog. But he also knew that Bar did not need a puppy. "Training puppies on your own rugs is a challenge. Training pups on government rugs is impossible." So George turned to his great friend Will Farish. Bar had fallen in love with my mother and sister in South Texas when she and George had joined Will and Sarah on a hunting trip after Christmas. Sarah had mentioned that my mother had had a big litter. So George called Will. Will said he was sure that he had a dog and called back later to ask if a girl would be all right. The Bushes had never had a female dog before,

but George said, "That would be great." Then Will called back and said he had the perfect dog . . . but she was liver-colored and white, not black and white like her beautiful mother and sister. George said, "Fine." So Will sent me to school to brush up on my manners. Remember, I had been a kennel dog for quite some time.

George was speaking in Cincinnati, Ohio, on the thirteenth of February, and then he and Bar were going to fly up to Maine for the weekend. Will brought me from Versailles, Kentucky, and we met the Bushes at the foot of the steps of *Air Force II*. It was love at first sight. Both Bushes kissed me and I sat on Bar's lap all the way to Maine. I'm going to be honest (this is a confession that is difficult for me to make and you will understand why as you read on). Bar did whisper to me that night, "You are *so* sweet, but you are *so* ugly. You have a pig's nose, you are bowlegged, and your eyes are yellow." I knew immediately that I was going to have to try harder. She also told me that she really loved me. I believed her. That was sort of a rocky start, but I have since heard her tell others that she will never have a male dog again and that I am the best dog they ever lived with. I believe that too.

The Vice-President's House is a big white Victorian house built in 1893. It sits on an eleven-acre tree-filled lot on a seventy-seven-acre circle of land known as the U.S. Naval Observatory. There is actually a working observatory on the grounds, an atomic clock, a map agency, etc., manned by approximately four hundred naval personnel. In the almost two years that we lived at the Observatory, I got to know and love almost all of them.

The gardens were very carefully tended by Mike and Beth. One day the first May I lived with the Bushes, a note from Beth to Laurie Firestone, my friend and Bar's superb social secretary, was put on Bar's desk. On it George had added his own memo—dated 5-13. The note read:

May 12 – Tues.

Dear Laurie,
We've got a problem: Millie is digging in and playing in some of the flower beds. Mike finished planting the bed on the slope near the rose garden yesterday afternoon. He had just enough plants to finish it. Millie dug a large hole, destroying a portion of the bed. We will have to re-order enough plants to re-do the bed. We have seen her playing and running through the edge of the long tulip bed before. We think that you and Mrs. Bush should be aware of this.

From the desk of
George Bush

5-13

Bar

Beth

This relates to your dog. Whatever has gotten into her?
GB

To Mike and Beth - I'm sorry.
"Millie"

Now that was funny as George hit tennis balls to me all the time . . . over the tulips, around the tulips, and *in* the tulips.

Bar made me apologize and send over a signed picture to the greenhouse.

I loved running on the grounds. I caught several squirrels, a possum, and chased a little red fox one night. George saw him racing across the lawn with his long red tail straight out behind him. He was so thin he ran through the fence. I ran into it.

There were trees to explore. I loved that too.

S peaking of trees at the Vice-President's House, one day in 1987, the U.S. Constitution's bicentennial year, we got a call to appear downstairs and out on the lawn. The National Arborist Association and the International Society of Arboriculture had come to put up a plaque by a big oak tree in the front of the house. This tree had been around since the signing of the Constitution. Every time we had a storm we all worried that this wonderful old tree with its swing would get struck by lightning

or be blown over. All the "grands" (as we call the grandchildren) loved that swing. In fact all children love it.
When we got downstairs we found five people under the
tree. They asked Bar to please gather the crowd, so she
asked Laurie Firestone, a secret service agent, and me to
step forward. A man read a long citation about the oak tree
and then Bar shook hands with them all and they left. Af-
terward I couldn't wait to see what that was all about. Several months later I read about the ceremony in their
national publication. From the pictures it looked like the
ceremony took place in front of a crowd of thousands.

everal months after I arrived at the V.P. House we got a letter from Benji, the famous dog movie actor, asking if he could come by for a courtesy call. He was on a tour promoting his latest movie. You can imagine my excitement. . . . I would get to meet a real live macho movie star. We invited two of the "grands," Jenna and Barbara, to bring over their Horace Mann kindergarten class to see the famous fella. He drove up in a big limousine, surrounded by aides, leaped out on command (as Bar pointed out), and then I discovered the awful truth. Benji turned out to be an aging (twelve-year-old) female. To add insult to injury, she also turned out to be the nicest, best-behaved, friendliest dog I have ever met. The next day the papers had a big article and picture of Benji visiting the U.S. Marine barracks with the marine mascot. I was barely mentioned. Not that I cared.

In the fall of 1987 Jenna and Barbara, George, Jr., and Laura's twins moved to Washington. Their dad decided to work full time in George's presidential campaign . . . no title, just as an ombudsman. And, according to Bar and George, his assistance was an enormous help and gift to his father. (It gets complicated in our family, for we have three Georges: George the father, George the son, and George the grandson. For purposes of clarification they will be known as George, "Junior" [although he isn't one], and George P.)

One night Junior and Laura were going out and Bar asked them if the twins could come for the night. All went well. They played outside, rolling down the Vice-President's lawn; they had dinner, took baths, and then George went upstairs to hear their prayers. When he got there, five-and-a-half-year-old Barbara was sobbing. Spikey, her stuffed cat, was missing and she told George that she just couldn't sleep a wink without Spikey. Jenna verified this horrid story by saying, "That's right, Gampy, she'll cry all night." George called Bar for help and they found out that Spikey had been with Barbara all over the house *and* grounds. Leaving Bar to comfort Barbara, George set out to search the house. . . . I went with him and we looked in every nook and cranny, to no avail. So we took to the outdoors. Now when a vice-president takes to the outdoors, a large contingent of secret service men goes with him. So there we were, searching the eleven acres of the grounds with flashlights . . . also to no avail. George said, as they went along, "I have work to do. What am I doing searching for a stuffed animal outdoors in the dark?" When we came back into the house Bar told George that Barbara had accepted another soft, snuggly animal and fallen asleep immediately.

The next morning when the drapes in the living room were pulled, there was Spikey. The girls had been hiding or playing house there. I, of course, knew where he was all the time, but I so enjoyed the hunt.

ery soon the campaign got going and those of us who stayed at home really felt left out. I was thrilled to be invited to a Republican Pet Fete. At the party I shared a chair with Box Car Willie Reagan, Maureen Reagan's dog. Blazer Lugar, Senator and Mrs. Lugar from Indiana's dog, and Congresswoman Helen Bentley's Baby Bleep Bentley from Maryland were also at our table. Posing for *Vanity Fur,* the stylish fashion magazine for dogs and cats, made me feel that I was giving my all for George. Don Rhodes, of course, chaperoned me at the party, because Bar said that a two-year-old is just not mature enough to go out alone on a date. And besides that, with names like Blazer and Box Car Willie, who knew what kind of boys they were? I thought that Mildred was a tough name for a dog. In this crowd, Mildred sounded very civilized.

I spent a lonely fall in 1988. The Bushes were off campaigning almost all the time. On November 8 when George was declared the winner, I got busy and decorated the house. Little did I know just exactly how much my life would change. For starters, Bar told me that I'd better get used to calling George "Mr. President," which I do some of the time . . . strictly for protocol purposes. I have permission to refer to him as "The Prez," also.

Shortly before President Ronald Reagan left office he described to George with some joy the collecting of nuts at Camp David, bringing them back to the White House, and feeding the squirrels outside the Oval Office. George said, "Oh gosh. Millie kills squirrels!" The President told George several days later that he'd thought about Millie and the squirrels, and that there was a place over by the First Ladies' Garden where he could put a run for Millie. George told the President that Bar'd never go for that. The last day that President Reagan was in office he asked George to step outside the Oval Office, and there was a sign . . . placed very low . . . so the squirrels could see it!

I wonder if George ever let President Reagan know that so far the score at the White House is eight known kills—that is, done in full sight of responsible people—four squirrels, three rats, and, to Bar's great sorrow, a pigeon.

On Inauguration Day 1989, I was in Kentucky at Lane's End Farm with Tug Farish. Tug is an absolutely adorable springer spaniel, chosen by Will Farish to be the father of my children. We got along like a house afire.

I stayed with Doug Drews, whom I have known from birth. Doug is really in charge of the garden at Lane's End, not in charge of visiting dogs who are in love. He drove me to Kentucky from the Vice-President's House and returned me to the White House. I felt that I'd missed all the excitement. But Bar tried on her inauguration gown for me to see. . . . Well, not quite true. She wore it the night they received the diplomatic corps at a white-tie reception in early February, and then the dress, her shoes, her stole, her famous "real" pearls, her earrings, and her beautiful evening bag went off to the Smithsonian for their permanent exhibit of First Ladies' gowns. I tried to act as though I didn't care about her dress at all.

The picture in the background is of little Miss Ruth Harding, no relation to President Harding. I overheard Lady Bird Johnson telling Bar that one day she was showing the family quarters to a group of visitors, and when she got to the Thomas Eakins picture of Ruth Harding, she said, "Have you ever seen a grumpier little girl? She really didn't want to have her picture painted, did she?" An elderly gentleman spoke up quietly saying, "You'll be glad to know that she improved when she grew up. I married her!"

This is just one of the many wonderful paintings in the White House collection.

Our life at the White House is pretty heavily scheduled. The alarm goes off at 6 A.M. The Prez says that I go off a few minutes earlier by shaking my ears pretty hard in their faces. In any case, Bar jumps up, throws on her clothes, and races down three flights of stairs, or takes the elevator if she feels a little tired. (She usually feels tired.) She walks me around the South Lawn drive, brings me back in, feeds me, and climbs back into bed to read the papers with The Prez and drink coffee and juice. Between 7 and 7:08, the President and I go off to the Oval Office.

I often sit in on the morning briefings.

I sometimes want to go out and hunt for squirrels.

I sometimes want to come in . . .

. . . to take a break.

The Prez says he gets pretty tired of letting me in and out.

As I was saying, our life is pretty scheduled. Almost every night Don Rhodes comes by to see The Prez, and then he takes me for a walk. I love Don and try very hard to be his friend. You've heard of a one-man dog? Well, Don is a one-dog man, I'm afraid. He was C. Fred Bush's best friend and always compares me to Freddy. I told Bar that I overheard him ranking dogs the other night. C. Fred, "Mr. Perfect," got a ten. I barely got a seven, and Ranger, one of my puppies, got a three, but he has a chance to improve. Bar told me not to worry, that Don really liked me. She said that I had to remember that Don still missed C. Fred.

She then told me a story about Don that explained it a little. Shortly after C. Fred died, The Prez told Don that they were expecting a new pup. It really hurt Don, for he thought they were going to forget C. Fred. He stuck his head into Bar's room and rather gruffly said could he ask her just one question? The question was, "If the Vice-President died, would you get a new husband?" Her answer didn't please him. She said, "You bet, if I could find one as good." She says he has only just now forgiven her. She also says that Don Rhodes is the best, most loyal friend that George Bush ever had, and that loyalty must be earned. I will just have to try harder.

I got pretty tired of waiting for Tug's and my babies. One of the Washington newspapers had a puppy watch giving a daily report on my condition. I had a needlepoint chin cushion and waited "like Patience on a monument."

One day in early March, Bar and I went to our dear friends Esther and Dick Moore's house for lunch. They surprised us with a puppy shower. The Moores knew something we didn't, for there were six of everything in the basket.

The White House has a fine family theater on the ground floor. The Prez likes to entertain there a lot. It looks here as though Lynda Robb (wife of the junior senator from Virginia) isn't sure she wants to sit next to Bar. Lynda Johnson Robb is great fun to invite to the White House, as she knows all sorts of interesting stories about it since she spent part of her growing-up years here.

Several days after the Robbs came to dinner and movies at the White House, the Bushes had another movie night. I felt funny all day long. I tried to make a nest outside in the garden. I tangled up my blanket. I just couldn't get comfortable. My tummy felt very full. Paula Rendon, the Bushes' beloved longtime housekeeper, came down to sit with me in my little birthing room. After dinner Bar excused herself from the guests and sat with me. She worked at her desk for a few minutes. I heard her call the doctor to ask what she should be doing. I was flabbergasted. You know I believe that she thought she was going to get into the act. At nine o'clock I sat up, took a few deep breaths, and lay down and had my first daughter. Bar called The Prez at the theater and told him that a

babe had come. About every fifteen minutes, a new pup arrived. At one time I heard George . . . whoops . . . the President ask her what they were, and Bar told him they were too young to tell and that they all looked alike. Then the last baby arrived. It was clearly different. I had produced five girls and one boy. To think that Bar thought she was going to help me when she couldn't tell a boy from a girl!

My babies were born in the little beauty parlor on the second floor. This beauty parlor was put in by Pat Nixon and has been used by every First Lady since, including Bar, in spite of what you hear, read, and see. The White House carpenters whipped up a marvelous nesting box (they'd made one before for President Ford's dog Liberty). Bar brought her desk into that room and worked there for

weeks before the babies were due. She was trying to get me used to it. I spent days waiting and waiting and waiting. Finally on March 17 and 18, my pups were born and I did have them in the proposed nest, although I would have preferred the Bushes' bed. Incidentally, my bed had a presidential seal on it. Theirs does not.

The babies grew and grew. At first they slept on shredded newspaper, but they got dirtier and dirtier from the ink. I'm afraid that Bar caused several newspapers great discomfort by mentioning publicly the fact that she enjoyed reading their newspapers, but hated the dirty ink. The Prez came to the rescue by getting rolls of unprinted paper for my babes. And that cleaned up their act considerably.

As the weather got better, they spent hours on the South Lawn playing and sleeping. We carried them down in a great plastic toy bag.

George . . . doggone it . . . the President took every opportunity to visit the pups.

He brought out delegations of people who visited him.

Sometimes he just sneaked out alone.

Sometimes he
played with
the pups.

S ometimes the pups were let out for big runs on the lawn. They liked that so much that sometimes we had to carry them back in.

I kept my eye on them.

When the pups were a month old, it was time for physicals and shots. Please note the lady who thought that she could help deliver the pups! Makes me wonder what kind of mother she was.

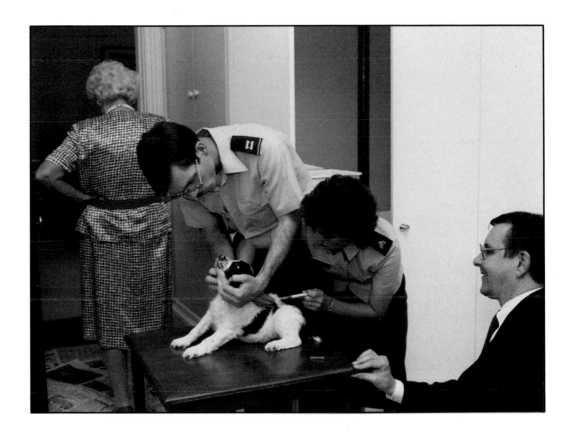

We started with six.

And then there were five.

Down it went to four.

A sad little three

A good little twosome

And finally a lonely little one

And, oh dark dog days, then there were none.

Although I love all the "grands," Marshall fast became a close friend. As soon as she could crawl, she'd get into my bed and I even let her play with my ball (translation: security blanket).

Marshall sat with me while I waited for the pups. Everyone knows that's a difficult time.

She was there almost immediately after the delivery.

Marshall visited the pups often.

So on her third birth-
day I gave her a puppy
. . . Ranger, my only son.
Ranger visits the
White House often.

One day in May, two of the pups stopped off in the China Room on the ground floor to be dried off. They'd been playing on the wet grass. They came upstairs and told me that they'd seen the most beautiful white dog in the room where samples of china used by the forty previous presidents are displayed. A week or so later, I thought I might just take a peek. Those silly pups . . . they'd seen Rob Roy, Calvin Coolidge's famous white collie, in a portrait . . . not in the flesh. That did give me an idea. All First Ladies have their portraits painted to be hung in the Grand Hall on the ground floor and adjacent rooms. This one is a portrait of Grace Coolidge done by Howard Chandler Christy. Dare I hope that Bar would consider having me in her portrait?

After the babies were old enough for me to leave them for extended periods of time, Bar and I walked over to the old Executive Office Building (the EOB) and visited the ladies and gentlemen in the mail room. The White House receives approximately 95,000 letters a month. Naturally The Prez gets the most, but for a while I was getting more than my fair share. So I went to say thank you very much. They even showed me my mailbox.

After the mail is sorted it gets sent out to many different offices in the White House. There were so many letters about my babies that the nice people in the mail room com-

posed a card from us that was sent out to everyone who wrote in. The babies and I signed also.

We so appreciated your warm welcome to Millie's puppies. All are doing well and we send our best wishes.

Barbara Bush

Gg Bush

Another day Bar and I went to call on the White House switchboard. These wonderful ladies can find anyone—anyplace. The Prez says, if the White House switchboard can't find them, they're no longer living.

May brought great honor to me. The babies and I were on the cover of *Life* magazine. I could only conclude that I was their selection for 1989 Mother of the Year. The babies and I looked smashing. I was glad to have a family picture before they all took off for new homes. If only Tug had been with us.

Just when I was riding high, out of the blue and with absolutely no provocation, the July 1989 issue of *The Wash-*

ingtonian magazine came out with their "Best & Worst" list. Guess whose picture was on the cover? Mine! Guess which I was . . . best or worst? Worst. The President advised me to "shake it off," ignore it, and not let it get my goat. It reminded him of the time that Dick Schaap (a sportswriter for *New York* magazine) wrote an article entitled "The Ten Most Overrated Men in N.Y.C." He told me that as the U.S. Ambassador to the United Nations his name headed the list. George invited the other nine men, the nervous author, and several ambassadors to a reception honoring "The Overrated." It was a great party.

The newspapers *and* the Bushes had lots of fun with *The Washingtonian* article. George immediately came to my defense. Bar was a little quieter. After what she had whispered to me that first night, I guess she felt this was one battle she should stay out of. The editors of *The Washingtonian* even apologized and sent me some marvelous dog biscuits. George accepted their apology. He wrote Jack Limpert, the editor of the guilty magazine: "Dear Jack: Not to worry! Millie, you see, likes publicity. She is hoping to parlay this into a Lassie-like Hollywood career. Seriously, no hurt feelings; but you are sure nice to write. Arf, arf for the dog biscuits—Sincerely, George Bush." Easy for the President to accept the apology. I did *not*. It was

Books for the Beach □ What It Costs to Dress Well
Inside the Style Section □ Discovering the Eastern Shore

WASHINGTONIAN

JULY 1989 $1.95

BEST & WORST

Our Pick as the Ugliest Dog:
Millie, the White House Mutt.
Plus the Best Veterinarians,
Sinful Desserts, Deejays, Diet
Drinks, Columnists, Beer, Pizza, Bagels, & More

bad enough to have my face on the cover, beside which they had written "Our Pick as the Ugliest Dog: Millie, the White House Mutt," but the picture they had inside was taken the very afternoon of my delivery. Show me one woman who could pass that test, lying on her side absolutely "booney wild" (family expression for undressed) on the day she delivered six babies!

I also objected to the word "mutt." I am a blueblood through and through. For starters, my dad came from the kennel of Sir John Thouron. Sir John's secretary very kindly wrote and offered my dad Tug's baby pictures for my book. In her letter she had one major piece of family news, and I quote: "One tragic item: Tug's younger brother, Guy, was given to a friend in Tallahassee where he was eaten by an alligator. So sad."

Well, *I'll* say that's sad!!

After *The Washingtonian* attack we got lots of letters. One of my favorites came from an eighty-two-year-old lady named Joy Fiske from Roseville, Minnesota. She enclosed a free-verse poem that she composed:

IN DEFENSE OF "UGLY MILLIE"

Barbara Bush, our First Lady
has a Springer Spaniel puppy
who was unjustly branded ugly
by the "Washingtonian Magazine" standards.
With Millie, beauty is more than fur deep.
How poor Millie must suffer
reading the writings of the Editor
of that prestigious magazine.

"Ugly Millie" chuckles to herself . . .
It is *she* who sleeps in the White House
It is *she* who eats the "Royal Chow"
It is *she* who knew her master's plan
of the trip to Beijing and Moscow.
The News writers of the "Washingtonian Magazine"

could not even guess
the inner strategy and timing.

"Ugly Millie" resting at
First Lady Barbara's knee
heard it all; could it be . . .
"Jealousy"?

Yes, many came to my defense. There were letters to the editor, and many letters sent directly to the White House. And, of course, the minute something gets into the computer, it keeps reappearing in print across the country. I guess the most pleasing message of all came directly from the office of Senator Bob Dole, who personally brought the following press release to the White House:

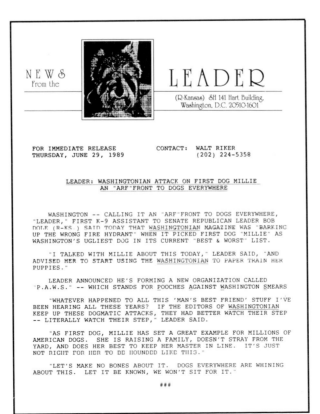

NEWS From the **LEADER**

(R-Kansas) SH 141 Hart Building, Washington, D.C. 20510-1601

FOR IMMEDIATE RELEASE   CONTACT: WALT RIKER
THURSDAY, JUNE 29, 1989   (202) 224-5358

LEADER: WASHINGTONIAN ATTACK ON FIRST DOG MILLIE
        AN "ARF"FRONT TO DOGS EVERYWHERE

    WASHINGTON -- CALLING IT AN "ARF"FRONT TO DOGS EVERYWHERE,
"LEADER," FIRST K-9 ASSISTANT TO SENATE REPUBLICAN LEADER BOB
DOLE (R-KS.) SAID TODAY THAT WASHINGTONIAN MAGAZINE WAS "BARKING
UP THE WRONG FIRE HYDRANT" WHEN IT PICKED FIRST DOG "MILLIE" AS
WASHINGTON'S UGLIEST DOG IN ITS CURRENT "BEST & WORST" LIST.

    "I TALKED WITH MILLIE ABOUT THIS TODAY," LEADER SAID, "AND
ADVISED HER TO START USING THE WASHINGTONIAN TO PAPER TRAIN HER
PUPPIES."

    LEADER ANNOUNCED HE'S FORMING A NEW ORGANIZATION CALLED
"P.A.W.S." -- WHICH STANDS FOR POOCHES AGAINST WASHINGTON SMEARS

    "WHATEVER HAPPENED TO ALL THIS 'MAN'S BEST FRIEND' STUFF I'VE
BEEN HEARING ALL THESE YEARS? IF THE EDITORS OF WASHINGTONIAN
KEEP UP THESE DOGMATIC ATTACKS, THEY HAD BETTER WATCH THEIR STEP
-- LITERALLY WATCH THEIR STEP," LEADER SAID.

    "AS FIRST DOG, MILLIE HAS SET A GREAT EXAMPLE FOR MILLIONS OF
AMERICAN DOGS. SHE IS RAISING A FAMILY, DOESN'T STRAY FROM THE
YARD, AND DOES HER BEST TO KEEP HER MASTER IN LINE. IT'S JUST
NOT RIGHT FOR HER TO BE HOUNDED LIKE THIS."

    "LET'S MAKE NO BONES ABOUT IT. DOGS EVERYWHERE ARE WHINING
ABOUT THIS. LET IT BE KNOWN, WE WON'T SIT FOR IT."

                          ###

One of the great myths . . . or misunderstandings . . . about people in public office has to do with gifts. The law says that the President (or any member of his family or any federal employee) may not accept a gift from a foreigner that is worth more than $180. The law also states that he or she must declare any gift he or she accepts from an American admirer that is valued at over $100 . . . and then he or she must be ready to accept the criticism and/or publicity that goes with it. For example: Bar accepted a perfectly beautiful watch from the Ladies of the Senate. She is so proud of that watch . . . not just because it is gold and beautiful, but because her dear friends gave it to her. She was president of the Ladies of the Senate for eight years when George was Vice-President, and she enjoyed it more than anything else she did. The wives of senators meet every Tuesday morning and work for the Red Cross, Children's Hospital, etc. No politics, just real friendship. That watch got lots of newsprint. Bar said she didn't mind, in fact liked the publicity, for it was a reminder of real friends.

I have been given the most generous assortment of gifts—collars, leashes, a sweater marked "Yale Bulldog" (why not "Yale Springer"?). I have a personalized seat belt . . . for when I go riding in a car, boat, or airplane. (The way George drives that boat, that's the only way I'd go out with him!) I have been given many dog bowls . . . mostly personalized, including a Waterford crystal one, and several biscuit jars filled with dog biscuits. We received many lovely T-shirts and sweatshirts that I assume are for Bar, and wonderful cushions and beds, almost one for every room. So kind.

Bar has been asked time and time again just how I got my name, and just who is Mildred Kerr? The Bushes have named all their children after best friends or beloved members of their families. They have named some of their animals the same way. Mildred Kerr is a dear friend of Bar's who lives in Houston, Texas. She told Bar that after *Life* came out with my picture on the cover as the 1989 Mother of the Year, people came up to her in the store and called her Millie or Mil . . . that is, people who had never, ever spoken to her before. Since Millie is not her nickname, she was very amused. The birth of the puppies even brought Mimi to Washington.

Bar got several letters from other Mildred Kerrs. One wrote: "May I ask why you named your dog after me? It is causing me some embarrassment."

The Kerr part of my name has caused *me* great embarrassment. Some people who just hear the name think that my name is Cur not Kerr.

The White House sits in the heart of the District of Columbia on 18.07 acres. I love running around these historic grounds. Every president since John Quincy Adams has planted a tree on the White House grounds. John's tree is looking a little poorly, but we are told that saplings from his tree are being saved for replacement purposes. That is the Adams tree directly behind me on the South Lawn. Incidentally, the Bushes think the South Lawn is their front yard.

The fountain on the South Lawn (below) was built in 1867 during the presidency of Andrew Johnson.

The fountain on the North Lawn was built during the presidency of Ulysses S. Grant in 1873. See the house behind me? It's white . . . except for where it's gray. The house is undergoing restoration for the 1992 bicentennial of the laying of the cornerstone. Now that the paint is off, visitors can see the blackened stone left over from the War of 1812 when the British set fire to the White House.

A secret: They know *when* the cornerstone was laid and they know *who* laid the cornerstone, but they don't know *WHERE* they laid the cornerstone.

Another secret, or little known fact, about the White House is that other than the two well-known gardens (the Rose Garden by the Oval Office, where so many official

ceremonies are held, and the First Ladies' Garden, where Bar has teas), there are two hidden, "secret" gardens. The one I like best is the Children's Garden, given as a Christmas present to the White House by President and Mrs. Lyndon Johnson. This sweet garden has a tiny little water-lily pond, and the names and hand- and footprints of the White House grandchildren in bronze are carefully set into the flagstones. Needless to say, the Bushes have the most grandchildren in the garden (twelve when this book went to print and more expected). The garden is best described in a letter Lady Bird Johnson wrote to the White House curator at that time. She writes:

> I've just walked down to see the tiny little garden which we want to leave for White House children and grandchildren of days to come.
> I like the way it's tucked away, and you're almost surprised to come upon flagstones leading through a "secret tunnel" lined by the holly trees. The apple tree will be

lovely, with blossoms in Spring, and fruit in Autumn and it's almost irresistibly "climable"! Wouldn't a small swing be nice there? I hope there will be some crocus among the flagstones for early Spring blooming.

I think of the spot as the sort of place a First Lady who is a grandmother might wheel a baby carriage and sit in the shade and enjoy her own back yard, in a quiet secluded spot. And very especially it would be a good place for four year olds to have a "tea party," or watch the goldfish in the little pool—or for their mother or grandmother to read about *Peter Rabbit* or *Winnie the Pooh*.

I shall think back affectionately about this dear House and these grounds we've loved these five years.

Lady Bird went on to thank the people who look after the White House for the "families who follow." The National Park Service takes magnificent care of the grounds. I love them and they seem to like liver-colored, yellow-eyed, bow-legged pig-nosed little girl dogs and never complain to Bar about my gardening.

This garden and the grounds may be seen during the spring and fall guided garden tours. They are usually held in mid-April and mid-October, depending on the President's schedule and the condition of the grounds and plants.

The other "secret" garden is right outside the Oval Office, and on a lovely day The Prez might have lunch out there or take some reading and do his work in this peaceful spot. This garden was created during the Reagan years and was a great gift to future presidents. This place is not on the garden tour.

The Bushes put in a horseshoe pit. The President has had spring and fall in-house horseshoe tournaments. Many a lunch has been skipped as teams qualify and matches are played. There is no happier sound than the clinking of a horseshoe as it hits the post. The Prez invited sixteen departments in the White House to field a team for the first tournament. It is now up to thirty-two teams and growing.

The horseshoe pit is right next to the swimming pool. Bar swims a mile almost every day. You talk about "watching grass grow"! That is, until the evening George called over to the residence and invited Bar and me to join him at 6:30. He said, "I am going to play horseshoes with Don and you can swim laps. Then we can all sit by the pool for

dinner." It was a beautiful night. I was sitting on the hill, hoping against hope that a squirrel would stroll by, when I heard loud screams. I raced back to the pool and found Bar pointing at a great big rat in the pool. She was swimming along when through her mask she saw a tremendous rat swim by, right in front of her. She says she doesn't know how she got out of that pool. She thinks that maybe she flew and she says that that rat did not look like Mickey Mouse. Thank heavens The Prez was there and stayed cool. He put in the pool scoop and got the rat in the net and did him in. I want to handle this gently because the agents are my friends. Let me put it this way, there *really* were quite a few other people there, but from where I sat, only the President dared get near that rat! The agents were protecting The Prez from a distance, a big distance. They claimed they were protecting from the enemy on the outside. The Prez was protected from the enemy on the inside. Inside, outside, all swimming ended for that day!

The White House pool was put in by friends of President and Mrs. Gerald Ford. The Bushes love the pool and have had cookouts, horseshoe tournaments, and swims all at poolside.

Almost every president has left something to the White House or made changes that make the house much more livable. The Truman Balcony is a joy. The Bushes have had lunch, served refreshments, and had dinner on the balcony. The Prez likes to bring heads of state there for a cup of coffee and a view of the monuments. The Jefferson Memorial is on a line with the White House. The Washington Monument is slightly off to the left. You can see the Potomac River on the horizon and airplanes landing across the river at National Airport. It is here that Bar and I often wave good-bye to the President or welcome him home. The helicopter lands on the South Lawn directly below the Truman Balcony.

Since we live on the second and third floors of the White House, you might well ask how I get up and downstairs. It's easy. I just ring the bell for the elevator and there's Roland or Woody. Woody knows the name of every single member of the family. Sometimes the family leave me outside, but Woody is always there. If The Prez is due to arrive, I can't get Woody to budge, but everyone else can wait for me.

The East Room at the White House is almost forbidden territory for me. This room has been used for a variety of purposes: Abigail Adams even dried the family laundry there. It's also been the scene of several great events, both joyful and sad, from weddings to funerals. It was here that President John Kennedy lay in state and President Richard Nixon gave his resignation speech. On a happier note, several presidents' daughters were married here, beginning with Maria Monroe and including Alice Roosevelt and Lynda Bird Johnson. The room is used primarily for entertaining and has been the site of hundreds of receptions and musical performances.

The grand piano in the East Room was presented to Franklin D. Roosevelt by Mr. Theodore Steinway, on behalf of the Steinway family on December 10, 1938. This was the 300,000th Steinway built. The gold-leaf decorations on

the grand piano represent American musical forms: a New England barn dance; a lone cowboy playing his guitar; the Virginia reel; two field hands clapping and dancing; and an Indian ceremonial dance. The three gilded mahogany legs are carved American eagles. Many great pianists have played on this piano. I'd sort of like to myself . . .

May 16, 1989, was a landmark day in the life of the Millie Bush family. It was a wet, very rainy Washington day, and my babies, Ranger and Camie, were restless. Their sisters had already gone on to their permanent homes. They couldn't go outside on the South Lawn, and so guess where they spent the morning? They were put in the East Room and all of the tourists got to see them. Do you think that I was invited to be with them in the "forbidden" room? Absolutely not.

As a matter of interest, about 125,000 people come through the White House each month, and about 1,500,000 come per year. The White House is opened to the public five days a week, Tuesday through Saturday, from 10 A.M. to 12 noon. Two of the four floors are shown on the tour, the ground floor and the state floor.

As I said, I'm not invited to the state floor very often. One day when I was banished to the upper regions of the White House, I got an urgent call to appear on the first floor for a formal reception. Casey Healey, Bar's personal assistant, told me that half the people going through the receiving line had asked for me or shown disappointment that they weren't going to see me, so Bar sent her to get me, although The Prez really doesn't like me to be at of-

ficial receptions. I came down the grand staircase and waited until I was noticed.

There were lots of "ohs" and "ahs" and I tried hard to get into as many pictures as possible. One lady who came through the receiving line gushed, "Well, the best thing that this administration has done is . . . Millie." I loved it, but later Bar told me that she was *silly;* many people who wait and wait in receiving lines forget what they want to say and out pops the first thing that comes to mind. Bar also claims that that woman went home and said to her husband, "I can't believe I said that stupid thing to the President."

After a while I got bored and went into the Green Room for a rest. Incidentally, the Green Room is where Bar receives the spouses of the heads of state after their formal arrival ceremony for a cup of tea and a little get-to-know-each-other chat. The chair I chose was the one where the spouses sit. The Prez says that this is just one reason why he does not want me to attend formal receptions.

I heard The Prez say later, "At least Millie stayed out of the Blue Oval Room." Oh . . . ?

Later I went into the Red Room. The shiny material is very comfortable. By the way, in the past few years the White House was accredited as a museum with honors under the very able leadership of its curator, Rex Scouten. I asked what "with honors" meant and was told in short order, "This means that you are *not* to sit on any furniture." (I was sorry I asked.)

The Red Room is next to the State Dining Room.

The State Dining Room sees a lot of action in the White House. I came down one morning to see how the setting-up for the state dinner for Australian Prime Minister and Mrs. Robert Hawke was going on. But I was way too early. Things were as usual; the James Monroe "gilded plateau with vases and figures" (the Vermeil Collection) running down the long dining-room table as it has since President Monroe bought it. The picture of President Lincoln that hangs over the mantel was painted by George Healey. This study of Lincoln was taken from a picture Healey had painted of Generals Grant and Sherman, Admiral Porter, and President Lincoln discussing peace on a Union steamer, *The River Queen*, on the James River near Rich-

mond, Virginia, toward the end of the Civil War. Four years after Lincoln died, Healey entered this painting in a White House competition for the best portrait of the fallen President. It did not win, but the Lincoln family liked it so much that they bought it. It was returned to the White House about sixty years ago. The original painting is in the President's office on the family floor in the White House. I often study it.

Under the Lincoln portrait on the mantel is the following prayer:

> I pray heaven to bestow
> The best of blessings on this house and all
> that shall hereafter inhabit it.
> May none but honest and wise men
> Ever rule under this roof.

The Hawke state dinner was to be our first dinner held outside in the Rose Garden, but Mother Nature was against us . . . 98-degree temperature and 98 percent humidity. It was a shame, as all my friends—the electricians, the carpenters, the flower shop, the ushers, the social office—just everyone connected to a state dinner had worked for several days to set up the Rose Garden. Tiny little white lights were intertwined down the staircases on the south side of the White House, through the hedges that lead to the garden, and all through the crab apple trees that line the garden. But all my friends said that it would be cruel and unusual punishment to ask people to attend a black-tie dinner outside in that heat.

Bar and I came down later that day to check the dining room. Everything looked very pretty. Nancy Clark, the brilliant head of the flower department, had done a really great job and her flowers looked lovely with the glorious Nancy Reagan china.

All that work was not lost. Two nights later The Prez entertained the Cabinet. It was a beautiful, cool, crystal-clear evening. Refreshments were served on the balcony outside the Blue Oval Room, and then the guests walked down the decorated staircase into the Rose Garden for dinner. It was a great fun evening for us all.

There are some won-
derful beds in the
White House on the
second floor. I have tried
them all. The Lincoln Bedroom has a large carved
rosewood bed. All the
guests ask for that room, of
course. All guests but the
President's brothers and
sister. Finally, after we had
lived in the house for six
months, they came to us
and asked if they'd be per-
mitted to buy a new mat-
tress for the bed. They said
it sagged toward the mid-
dle, and did we know it
was made of horsehair? I
thought it was very com-
fortable and couldn't understand their attitude. However,
since Lincoln never slept in either the bed or the bedroom,
the mattress had no historic importance, so the Bushes
gladly said yes.

Until 1902 this room was an office. It was in this very
place that the Emancipation Proclamation was signed. As
for the bed, it was bought from a Philadelphia retailer in
1861 to be used in the principal guest room in the Lincoln
White House. History tells us that President and Mrs. Theodore Roosevelt and President Woodrow Wilson did sleep
in this beautiful bed.

There is a handwritten copy of Lincoln's Gettysburg
Address on a desk in the Lincoln Bedroom. President Lincoln copied the speech five times to benefit a charity for
Civil War soldiers. He signed the fifth and final copy. It is
this copy that is in the White House.

Although this is the room where the White House ghost

91
◇
MILLIE'S
BOOK

is supposed to appear, the Bushes have not seen it, nor do they believe in ghosts. I must confess that I have not seen one either. I liked hiding my rawhide bones in this room, but George followed me down the hall one night and caught me. He said he got tired of buying me new bones and he wanted to know just what I was doing with them. There behind the green curtains he found my cache. So, of course, I have now taken to hiding them in couches and chairs all over the second floor.

The Queens' Bedroom is truly the prettiest guest room in the White House. During the twentieth century, this room has served as a guest room for many distinguished female guests. Called the Rose Guest Room until it was refurbished in 1962 by Mrs. John Kennedy; she renamed the room because it had been occupied by many royal guests. Just to name a few:

Queen Elizabeth of Great Britain (now the Queen Mother) in 1942
Queen Wilhelmina of the Netherlands in 1942
Queen Juliana of the Netherlands in 1952
Queen Frederika of Greece in 1953
and Queen Elizabeth II of Great Britain in 1957

The high-poster mahogany bed in the Queens' Bedroom is reported to have belonged to Andrew Jackson. I like this bed very much . . . sometimes on top . . . and sometimes underneath.

Most of the paintings in the Queens' Room are portraits of ladies. I overheard Bar telling a guest that the Thomas Sully painting in the Queens' Bedroom was of a famous British actress and writer, Fanny Kemble. Her portrait hangs in the White House because she visited the mansion during Andrew Jackson's presidency. The guest, knowing that Andrew Jackson was a widower, asked just how often she had visited. But Bar stopped that rumor quickly. Fanny Kemble was highly esteemed by nineteenth-century Americans and was honored at the White House with a reception. Her nephew later married President Ulysses Grant's daughter, Nellie, in the Blue Room.

One rumor that Bar couldn't stop was the story that Rachel Jackson died of a heart attack while trying on a gown for the Inaugural Ball. She is said to have overheard two ladies in the next dressing room discussing her suitability as the First Lady. The nation's capital was full of gossips saying that Rachel had not been divorced from her first husband when she married Andrew.

Bar says her favorite portrait is in the Queens' Bedroom. It amuses her. It is of Lucy Payne Todd, wife of an associate justice of the United States Supreme Court and the sister of Dolley Madison. Bar says, "You know how you hope a portrait will flatter you? Well, here sits Lucy, thinning hair, five o'clock shadow, and double chins." Bar asks, "If this picture flatters Lucy, what do you think Lucy *really* looked like??"

Lucy was the first bride in the White House. She was the sister to whom Dolley wrote describing fleeing from the White House before the British arrived. That's how we know that Dolley rescued the Gilbert Stuart portrait of George Washington by cutting the canvas from the frame, rolling it up, thus saving it from being burned with the house and other furnishings.

Halfway down the center hall, opposite the Yellow Oval Room, is a cross hall with two lovely bedrooms and two baths.

One bedroom is used for the "grands" (who would much rather be on the third floor, out of Bar's first strike zone) and the other is used for guests. The bed in this room is VERY comfortable. I'm told that Presidents Johnson, Nixon, and Carter all slept in this bed. I can certainly see why.

The Yellow Oval Room has a very exciting history. It was a family library for that rambunctious Teddy Roosevelt family. Presidents Franklin Roosevelt, Dwight Eisenhower, and Harry Truman used it for their White House offices. It was here that President Roosevelt received the news of the attack on Pearl Harbor, and all during World War II the room was filled with maps and charts.

Surely one of the nicest uses of this room was the day Casey Healey called to ask "a big favor." She was picking up her wedding dress nearby and asked if she could borrow a room in the White House so she could have a wed-

ding picture taken for the Oklahoma papers. So into the Yellow Oval Room we went. I couldn't understand it. The tears flowed and Bar said it was because she loved this lovely young woman, couldn't go to her wedding, and because she was *so* happy for her. All of these things were true for me and I didn't cry. I do not understand Bar!

Today this lovely room is used for formal visits from heads of state and their wives, and for upstairs receptions, and Bar has used it for a lovely private luncheon for sixty. (The luncheon was to have been on the Truman Balcony, but once again Mother Nature did not cooperate and sheets of rain came down.) So, the luncheon moved inside and the Bushes discovered the most beautiful dining area in the White House.

Bar says that that is not quite true. In 1960 when Mrs. Kennedy moved into the White House, she found that there was no upstairs dining room. The family ate on trays or on makeshift tables and areas around the second floor. She took two bedrooms on the north side of the house and converted them into a very utilitarian kitchen and a truly glorious dining room with historic wallpaper. This room can seat forty at four round tables, and the Bushes gave their first party for the Secretary General of the United Nations and Mrs. Perez de Cuellar in this room.

The long center hall has also been used for dining. A favorite Bush way to entertain is to have a buffet dinner set up in the dining room and eaten in the hall before a movie is shown. At each end of this long hall are two sitting rooms: the little East Sitting Room, where guests from the Queens' Room and the Lincoln Bedroom might meet for breakfast, and the West Sitting Room, where Bar often has briefings or where guests might meet informally before dinner.

There is a lovely room on the second floor that has at various times been a bedroom or a presidential office that the Bushes have made into their family sitting room. It is here that they sometimes watch the evening news or curl up with a good book. Most of the furnishings in this room belong to the Bushes and were literally picked up from the upstairs sitting room at the Vice-President's House and were in place in the White House the third day after the inauguration. This is the twenty-ninth move for them and Bar says it is the first one that they have ever made where absolutely nothing had to be done. Nancy Reagan left the White House sparkling and totally furnished. On the twentieth of January, twenty-eight members of the family moved into a perfect house.

The canvas for the needlepoint rug in the family sitting room was painted by Aileen Sterling Crawford. Bar started it in China in 1975 and finished it at the Vice-President's House in 1983.

The hanging over the fireplace is part of a Chinese robe that the Bushes bought when they lived in Beijing in 1974. They had it stretched and framed when they got home.

I believe the President's favorite room in the White House is his upstairs office. This room is directly across from the grand staircase, and visitors may be led right up and into his office without having to run through all the booby traps set by the "grands" or by Bar and her friends. At different times in history this room has been the office of the President (Theodore Roosevelt, Franklin Pierce, etc.), the Cabinet Room, the Monroe Room (during the Hoover administration, it became a sitting room containing objects from the Monroe period), and the Treaty Room (the peace treaty with Spain was signed in this room on August 12, 1898).

The President has filled this room with comfortable furniture and paintings. It is here that George Healey's "The Peacemaker" hangs. The Prez and I admire this painting and are inspired when we look at it. He is so inspired by it that when he addressed the forty-fourth session of the

United Nations General Assembly, he said:

"There's a painting that hangs on the wall of my office in the White House and it pictures President Abraham Lincoln and his Generals meeting at the end of a war that remains the bloodiest in the history of my country. Outside, at the moment, a battle rages—in this picture. And yet what we see in the distance is a rainbow—a symbol of hope, of a passing of the storm. That painting is called *THE PEACE-MAKERS*. For me, it is a constant reminder that our struggle—the struggle for peace—is a struggle blessed by hope."

Many other paintings in the President's residence office are of the West, to remind him of his beloved Texas, and of the sea, to remind him of the rugged coast of Maine that he so loves.

Speaking of Maine, there are two wonderful places in our lives that I have not mentioned. One is, of course, Kennebunkport. It is here that the Bushes get together with family. Not just their children and grandchildren, but their mother, aunts, uncles, and cousins by the dozens. They love them all and it is ''controlled chaos,'' to quote Marshall's dad. A more perfect description I never heard.

They compete in everything: Pegity, horseshoes, tennis, swimming, boating, stickball, and fishing for the wily mackerel or elusive big bluefish.

Bar and The Prez love Kennebunkport. She is a newcomer, of course, having only come there for forty-six years. George, on the other hand, has come to Kennebunkport every year of his life since he was born except

for the year he was overseas during World War II. So not only his family are there, but also his friends. Now his friends' children and grandchildren are playing with his.

The "grands" climb the rocks by the hour. They race around in plastic coupes, helicopters, and scooters. It's here they learn to ride two-wheelers. It's here they learn to share. It's here they learn to sit through a sermon at little St. Anne's Church. Here they don't have to eat their vegetables. They may just say, "No, thank you," and never eat another bite. It's here that they learn to break that rule along with every other rule their grandmother makes. It's here they get to know their Great-Ganny, The Prez's precious mother. It is here that they learn a lot about the great worth of family, faith, and friends.

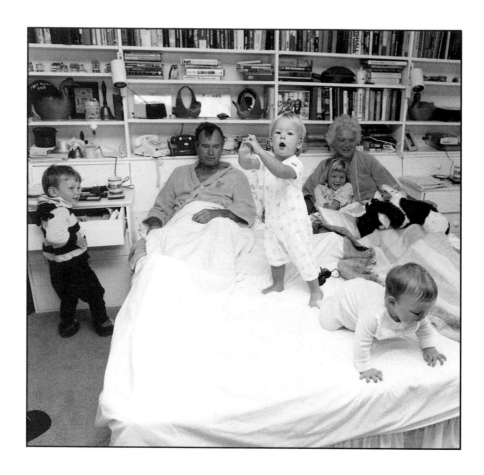

This is naturally *not* my favorite place in the world. First of all, I do not want to share Bar and George with anyone. Why, I can hardly find room in my own bed in the morning, not to mention theirs. Every grandchild comes down in the morning and climbs in. Second, there is not a squirrel in the place. Groundhogs and skunks abound. I can't catch the former and, to my great sorrow, I did catch two of the latter. I detest the boat and have been dragged on twice. The Prez says, "Never again." Who's arguing? So I spend lonely hours on the wall waiting for them to return.

The best place in the world is Camp David. Absolutely no cameras are allowed there, so no pictures. But although we do have guests at Camp David, for the most part I am allowed to join in on all activities. I jog with the President. I go to his office and work in the mornings. I referee the horseshoe matches. I watch the bowling, tennis, golf, and swimming. I watch movies. I take long nature walks. I protect Bar and The Prez from the deer that feed down the hill outside our cottage. I give them a half-hearted chase. I spend hours watching the goldfish in the pond. *And* there are squirrels by the hundreds. I love Camp David.

No book written by a Bush dog would be complete without a chapter on name-dropping. The late C. Fred Bush wrote in his book that he considered "name-dropping an art." Remember that we class name-droppers *never* say, "I know . . . [let's say] . . . Henry Kissinger." Rather we say, "Henry Kissinger knows me." There's sort of a subtle nuance there we like.

Well . . . Henry Kissinger does know me.

And here are a few others also who know me or my pups:

Kings and Queens
Presidents and those who would be Presidents
Astronauts
Governors
Princes and Princesses
Actresses and Actors
Members of Congress
(including the great Speaker of the House)
Senators and Athletes
(and some Senators who are also Athletes)
Big Shots
Democrats and Republicans
Members of the Press
Heads of State and their Wives
Secretaries of State
National Security Advisors
Religious Leaders
Friends

They all know me or my pups.

I overheard the Bushes talking the other night. Some discussion about me keeping a lower profile. The media were reporting that I was getting more publicity than some members of the Cabinet. Considering some of my press, maybe they should be grateful.

I could not finish my book without telling you a little about my pups, where they are and how they are faring. They all grew up loving flowers. I know they inherited that from me. They spread across the country. My daughter Camie lives in Miami, Florida, with George P., Noelle, and Jebby. My daughter Spot Fletcher went to live in Texas with Jenna and Barbara. (Spot was named after Scott Fletcher, who played for the Texas Rangers and was a favorite of the girls. As luck would have it, he was traded away and so the pup is now called Spot. I still think of her as Spot Fletcher.) Spot is a big Texas Ranger fan. My daughter Bar lives at Lane's End in Kentucky and has risen to unexpected heights. She has met and been hugged by Queen Elizabeth II of Great Britain. My daughter B.J. lives in Virginia with the Domingo Quicho family. She stays in touch and comes back to see me, but not often enough. My daughter Lady lives with Bernie and Patty Presock, who adore her, and Ranger lives with Marshall, so I see him often. It is true that I love to see them come visit and it is even truer that I love to see them go home.

One final thing I'd better make clear. I know the Bushes love me. They told me so. But they love people more, *all* people. So I have written this book and the proceeds will go to help people, *all* people. I hope it will strengthen families and family life in our great America.

The Prez used to tease Bar and tell her that if she'd "stick with him, he'd show her the world." And he did.

The Prez told me that if I'd stick with him, he'd show me my name in a *THOUSAND POINTS OF LIGHT,* and he did.

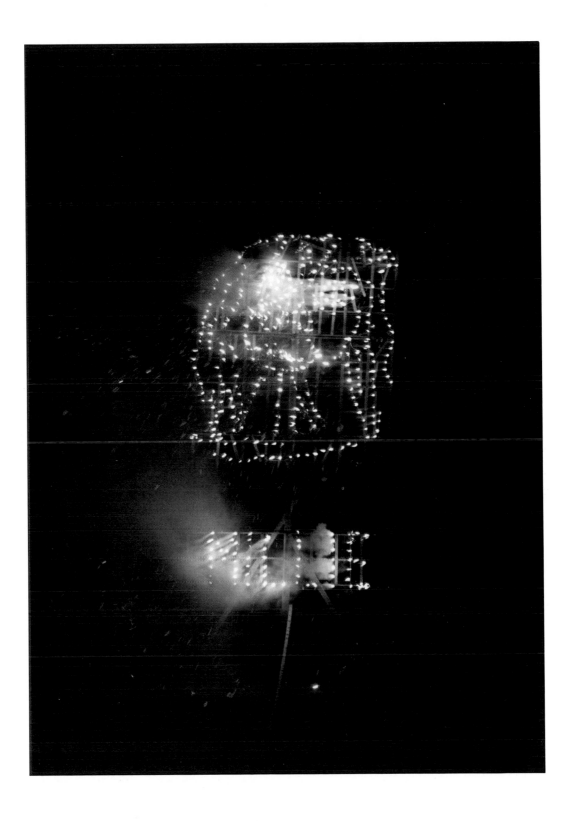

These people appear on the following pages:

139
◇

Grateful acknowledgment is made to those photographers whose work appears on the following pages:

Susan Biddle: 30, 32, 40, 44, 46, 47, 52, 57, 59, 79, 83, 89, 105, 124, 125 *top*, 126 *top*, 133.

Barbara Bush: 17, 24, 39, 119 *top*.

Doug Drews: 26.

Adelle Hall: 76.

Linda Kaye: 134 *top*.

Carol T. Powers: 25, 31, 35, 37, 38, 41, 48, 50–51, 53, 54, 55, 58, 60 *bottom*, 61 *top*, 62, 64, 65 *bottom*, 70, 73, 74, 75, 77, 80, 81, 84, 85, 86, 87, 88, 90, 91, 92, 93, 94, 95, 96, 99, 100, 109, 113 *top*, 114 *bottom*, 115 *bottom*, 118, 119 *bottom*, 120 *top*, 121, 125 *bottom*, 126 *bottom*, 127 *bottom*, 128 *top*, 129, 130, 131, 134 *bottom*.

Michael Sargent: 36, 42–43, 45, 61 *bottom*, 112, 114 *top*.

David Valdez: 10, 11, 12, 15, 16, 18, 19, 21, 27, 28, 29, 33, 49, 56, 60 *top*, 72, 101, 102–103, 104, 107, 108, 110, 111, 113 *bottom*, 115 *top*, 116, 117, 120 *bottom*, 122, 123, 127 *top*, 128 *bottom*, 137.

And to:

Life cover photograph by William Wegman: 66.

Vanity Fur photograph by Jeffrey Markowitz: 22–23.

Washingtonian for use of cover: 67.